When I Think On Your Lives

When I Think On Your Lives

Tara Kainer

Hidden Brook Press

First Edition

Hidden Brook Press
www.HiddenBrookPress.com
writers@HiddenBrookPress.com

Copyright © 2011 Hidden Brook Press
Copyright © 2011 Tara Kainer

All rights for poems revert to the author. All rights for book, layout and design remain with Hidden Brook Press. No part of this book may be reproduced except by a reviewer who may quote brief passages in a review. The use of any part of this publication reproduced, transmitted in any form or by any means, electronic, mechanical, photocopied, recorded or otherwise stored in a retrieval system without prior written consent of the publisher is an infringement of the copyright law.

When I Think On Your Lives
by Tara Kainer

Editor – Elizabeth Greene
Cover Art – Néle Azevedo
Author Photographs – Daniel Araquiel Dietzel
Cover Design – Richard M. Grove
Layout and Design – Richard M. Grove

Typeset in Garamond
Printed and bound in USA

Library and Archives Canada Cataloguing in Publication

Kainer, Tara Lynn, 1952-
    When I think on your lives / Tara Kainer.

Poems.
ISBN 978-1-897475-68-3

    I. Title.

PS8621.A4635W54 2011   C811'.6   C2011-902445-4

for my family

Contents

I: Celestial Convergence

Prologue – *p. 2*
Celestial Convergence – *p. 3*
Dreaming the Muse – *p. 4*
A Reminder – *p. 5*
On Becoming the Other – *p. 6*
On the Threshold – *p. 7*
I Think of David Suzuki – *p. 8*
Periplum – *p. 10*
Contrasts – *p. 12*
A Single Seed – *p. 14*
Natural Desires – *p. 16*
The Legacy – *p. 18*
Respite – *p. 19*
A Conversation of Crows – *p. 20*
In a Word – *p. 21*
It's Fitting We're Leaving – *p. 22*
Testimonial – *p. 24*
Four Short Poems:
    1. Wind – *p. 27*
    2. New Moon – *p. 27*
    3. Vines – *p. 27*
    4. Sadness – *p. 27*
Late Bloomer – *p. 28*
I Didn't Count On This – *p. 30*

II: The Trace in the Mind

Prototype – *p. 34*
Haiku – *p. 35*
Hast 'ou seen the rose – *p. 36*
Hunger – *p. 37*
A Lunatic's Love Song – *p. 38*
The Trace in the Mind – *p. 39*
"de mis solidades vengan" – *p. 40*
The Homecoming – *p. 41*
You Couldn't Have Known – *p. 42*
Denial – *p. 43*
Love is like death – *p. 44*
Logos – *p. 45*
Bonded Not – *p. 46*
Desert Bloom – *p. 47*
This Yearning – *p. 48*
Triptych – *p. 50*
There's a Funeral Here Today – *p. 54*
Elegy – *p. 55*
I Believe in a Power Greater Than Myself:
    It's Not Always Kind – *p. 56*
Past Hope – *p. 57*
Dreams – *p. 58*
Weather – *p. 59*

III. When I Think On Your Lives

When I Think On Your Lives – *p. 63*
Collateral Damage: April 2003 – *p. 64*
Telling Stories – *p. 70*
First Memories – *p. 71*
Misreadings – *p. 72*
At the Laundromat – *p. 74*
As You Turn – *p. 75*
At the Post Office – *p. 76*
A Matter of Time – *p. 78*
Desire Being Their Birthright – *p. 80*
Self-Doubt – *p. 82*
At the Welfare Office – *p. 83*
Remember the Days – *p. 85*
But I'm Hungry – *p. 86*
They Picked Up My Son – *p. 88*
On the Beach – *p. 90*
On Your Birthday – *p. 91*
It's the Laughter – *p. 93*

Notes to the Poems – *p. 96*

Acknowledgements – *p. 99*

Biographical Sketch of Author – *p. 100*
Biographical Sketch of Cover Art Artist – *p. 101*

I
Celestial Convergence

Lucky is he who has been able to understand the causes of things.
— Virgil, Georgics No. 2

The aim remains: to understand the world.
— John Bell, Irish Physicist

Prologue

> *The artist is always beginning.*
> — Ezra Pound

Where does one step into the stream?
At which point do I say, Be still.
A backwards flow into memory,
Landscape already altered,
Shadows cast, images
In sharp relief,
Details put down so others may live:
Act of creation a certain death.

Celestial Convergence

> *What could be more perfect than the moon?*
>   – Andre Dubus, <u>Voices From the Moon</u> (1984)

On opposite ends
of the horizon

planets are pearls
stranded
       in indigo sky:

Saturn, Mercury, Jupiter,
       dazzling Venus,

all beckoning
to that spun-butter moon.

       I, here below,
             am anchored

       to this pedestrian Earth, head

       tipped back
             to the heavens:

       moonstruck.

Dreaming the Muse

Beautiful dark dream full
of shadows and golden light

primordial forces, stark
stone structures, a choir

of mournful voices. Hands
grope in the night for the form,

feel its immensity and
strength, trace the pattern:

two grooves in the towering stone
pillar, indentations worn smooth

and soft by time. Intertwining,
spiralling, the progression

of a melody, two voices murmuring
and manifested in stone. Fingers

release the music, notes fly
free like birds long-caged.

Slow and deliberate the chant.
In the cavernous temple

firelight flings shadows
against corners of grey stone.

A Reminder

Stripped to the elements:
water, rock, sky,
                air

I the intruder, even
trees an overlay,
feature
                added,
like an extra layer
of paint on the artist's
canvas

Water wearing on rock,
      rocks dissolving
      into water, air
rushing at both, sky
a mirrored dome
cradling all

And then the other —
drip of paint or
      slash on canvas;
an undeniable feature
coiling inexorably
      into existence;
there, for all time,
      a reminder

On Becoming the Other

Divided from the canopy of sky,
disconnected from the garden

where moments before
I had plunged my toes

and felt them root deep
like the tendrils of flowers, hear

the dry rasp of the bleached out corn
stalks crescendo into a chorus

of jeers, your mocking whispering voice
slithers to the underside of the solitary

tree, is swept up into frenzied
movement of sunshine and shadow.

Again that voice:
not-sea, not-sky, not-earth
neither tree nor flower.
Yes, I concede,
I'm what is left over
once everything else has been named.

On the Threshold:
upon reading the latest research

So that's not true, either:
Loons do not mate for life
Brontosaurus never lived

And Sphinx - quintessential
Egyptian mystery – predates
That culture.

                    I inhabit a world
That does not exist, never did,
Feel my way across the surface

Fragile as egg shells
Illusory as light
Insubstantial and hollow as words.

                Caught here
Between what's gone and what will be,
Future worlds discredited

By past mistakes,
Exiled from the moment, out of
Reach and beyond redemption

Cognizant of ambiguous gain
Bringing
                nothing
But hidden losses

I Think of David Suzuki

I think of David Suzuki
when I'm too busy to walk the twenty
steps to the recycling bin, too lazy
to sort paper from cardboard and throw
both into the garbage instead. I think
of you, Dr. Suzuki, when I can't cram
another thing into the compost pail
under my sink, don't get outside
to empty it and put the organic scraps,
 yes, again, into the garbage.
You're not smiling. Eyes grim
behind your glasses, I think of you
as I drive my car to the store
when I could have easily walked instead,
buy fresh New Zealand lamb chops,
California strawberries, green peppers
from Mexico, decide the twisty,
environmentally-friendly florescent
light bulbs can wait, even though
I clearly see you, smiling, on a billboard
holding one in the palm of your hand.
I feel guilty when you remind me
my ecological footprint is growing,
let the water gush while I brush my teeth;
catch you frowning as I peel potatoes,
contently watch clean water spiral
down the dirty drain. I think of you
as I let the shower run & run
because it's so warm
in the chilly morning, so cool
in the summer heat, because

it's washing away all the grime
of the city, the cares of my day, the
fear that we've really done it now: it's
the hottest year yet, coming on the heels of
the hottest years in history; we're suffering
through another smog day, and I'm finding it
difficult to breathe. We're at the tipping point,
facing extinction and taking the planet with us.
I think of you and I'm afraid.

Periplum

> *Periplum, not as land looks on a map*
> *But as sea bord seen by men sailing.*
> — Ezra Pound, Cantos.

One cool summer's night lying
on our backs in the wet grass,

cold seeping through our clothes
and numbing our shoulders,

we stared side-by-side and silent
into a night so clear stars

spilled like milk across the sky,
but I picked out the patterns

as well as I knew them, Big Dipper,
Cassiopoeia, and Sirius the Dog Star.

Albebaron (or was it Mars) glowed
red. My mind took its place

beside the crescent moon and
hung there a-
                mazed.

We stayed there communing
with the heavens and each other

our bodies penetrated by the celestial
fire. How sublime this garden of stars,

my mind stretched to contain its borders
Measuring the light of my mind

by the light of those stars, charting
the constellations of my being.

Contrasts

Winter never rots in the sky.
— 17th C. proverb.

For me,
a winter's day
      in Saskatchewan

cattle huddled
   against the wasteland
   round the iced
   over trough,
breath billowing
   in gauzy balloons
   above their heads,

sparrows clinging
   to the chimney's
      edge

and bare branches
scratching at lighted
windows for warmth

      You were born
in the bloom of summer
amongst ripening fruit trees
perfumed breezes
      wafted over
           your cradle and wind
sang lullabies to the nodding
           stars

    Stalwart as the oak
lithe as the bending willow
        sun dancing
    in your sea-blue eyes
          laughter
                  breaking
like waves against the shore

    Your heart is a garden
    With the larks you exult

      While I stand here
             glowering
    through a cage
of blighted branches
    composing dirges
    for a murder
      of crows.

A Single Seed

After a morning in the garden
hands stained with the scent
of basil, cilantro, and mint,
busy in the kitchen I stop
amazed to think
what brought me here
from that initial word
or sound or
point of light -
that intelligence
unfurling or hurtling
toward the edges of being, how
did I arrive at this place,
to this intersection of space
and time, why did it catch me
up, land me here
in this particular location
at this precise moment.

I am
a middle-aged woman
of the 21st century. Three
children, three jobs, alone
in a rented apartment, an image
in the mirror I don't recognize.
What convergence of forces
rooted me here? Which corner
should I have turned, thought
suppressed, action taken, lover
embraced?

I am stupefied suddenly
stand stark still
with the enormity of this moment -
a single seed in the beginning
held infinity, all futures imaginable
some actualized, others yet to be.
Yet I am here
in my kitchen
blanching beans and zucchini,
washing lettuce and boiling brine,
building stores against the future.

Natural Desires

I want to be able
to say the word
STONE
      feel it smooth
      and heavy
      on my tongue
           drop
              it
                  from
            my mouth
               whole

      and measure
      its weight
            as
                    it
             falls

I want to utter
BIRD
      have its wings unfurl
           and
      take flight
      straight for the sun

      not grope
      towards the light
      of this shadowy world
      stop cold
      at the boundaries
      I can't cross over

I want to name things
know what things are
      want *grass*
to sprout before my eyes
to spring up tall and green
sway gently in the wind

Before my mind's eye
that tiny orange flower
fluttering in the breeze
like licks of fire:

overweening desire
for that flower
to burst into flame
to come alive

      here
on the page

The Legacy

Even the scar that lies
across my back
like a small silver fish
elongated and iridescent
was a glancing blow
quickly healed and forgotten

Wounds of the spirit
are immaterial
blaze bright as light
never fade
and disobey
all laws of the flesh
imprisoning them
lurk just behind the eyes
take refuge deep inside the gut
run along the nerves of the body
are imprinted on every cell

Had I a daughter
I'd have passed them on
to her, like instincts

Respite

> *Some happy tune*
> *Of meditation, slipping in between*
> *The beauty coming and the beauty gone.*
>   – *Most sweet it is,* William Wordsworth (1835)

Such a comforting shade

of brown this inbetween

state is. Like sepia ink

on a wash drawing

dark pool at the centre

drawn imperceptibly

toward the edges of being.

Waves lapping at the shore.

So gentle the slap of the water.

Not to be drawn out to sea

or cast upon the land. O *the mind,*

mind has mountains — but

to tumble so slowly, so

slowly and gently, to be

lulled, here, at the shore.

A Conversation of Crows

Solitary crow calls to his friends across the road.

They answer with a cacophony of caws, hop
excitedly from branch to branch, or send salutations
in stiff unsynchronized bows by tipping their bodies
back and forth in slow motion.

Perched high on a spruce limb too slight
for his weight and flapping wings furiously
to stay alight, lone crow punctuates each
movement with a string of cursing caws.

Picking beans in the garden I wonder what the ruckus is,
strain to hear the ten different calls Ernest Thompson Seton
identifies in crow language, fail to hear anything
but   Caw!   Caw!   Caw!

They're communing, though, those crows, batting caws
back and forth like a ping-pong ball, sometimes rising
emphatically at the end of a phrase or exclamation, or
descending in a gentle curve to frame a question mark.

Now they're lined up in a row like ellipses or a series
of dashes while my friend over here, confident now, keeps
to his branch, springs up and down at the tip of his board
ready now, to dive headlong into the conversation.

In a Word

The wandering earth herself may be
Only a sudden flaming word.
— W.B. Yeats, "The Song of the Happy Shepherd" (1889)

Why try to make one word follow another

        when really

      they shoot out

    like sparks from a fire
        or twist

crazily
    across the landscape

    grass bending before the wind.

    A word

is ripe fruit hanging from branches, light
    winking through trees, the uni-

      verse

    hurtling away from its still dark centre.

Words tumble and leap like swiftly moving rivers

      explode into sound

      or lie

      still and heavy

        as stone.

    Why march them
    one after the other
    in neat, straight lines
    stiff and erect
    as soldiers?

It's Fitting We're Leaving

It's fitting we're leaving
in this pouring rain,

dark mountains rising
like slag heaps

out of mist and fog,
rolls of gossamer

cloud settling heavily
down mountainsides.

In the best of weather
dazzling sunlight

reflecting off corrugated,
snow-covered peaks

against a backdrop
of surreal-blue sky,

they are menacing. *Here
we are, they shout. Solid*

*in our grandeur, inviolable
in our mass.* Falls roar

down precipices into canyons,
solid fortress of black-green fir

forms cover for grizzles, haven
for cougars and rattlers.

My response is visceral, a
tightening of innards,

restriction of breath.
How I miss the long release

of prairie, ubiquitous sky an
 invitation to breathe and feel

and think, an opening
for lungs and heart and mind.

Testimonial

How long since I've stood
Here, my eyes seeking
The space between mainland
And island, drawn to that openness
Where sea and sky meet.
Somewhere land closes off
The waters on the others side; still,
This lake is capable of an ocean's
Meanness, host to direful blasts and
Lashing waves, sudden storms
Whipping up a boiling roil of water,
Froth striking against boulders,
Deafening roar of thunder and wave,
Indifferent forces that wreck our lives,
have drowned full many a midnight ship
with all its shrieking crew.

Today the water's a gently heaving bosom,
Even the rocks seem to breathe, my
Corresponding breath blowing out
To meet the quiet tug and pull, a
Simultaneous sigh of air and wave, of
Motion thrown back upon itself, a
Moment suspended before the next
Intake, or gasp.

Slick sheet of surface blue
Masks any evidence of past dangers,
Invisible reefs, subterranean shoals
Or any potential fury to drown
Sailors and down ships, 10,000

All-tolled, they say, sunken treasures
All - archaeological digs bearing testimony
To Kingston shipwrights and engine founders,
To the grace of 19th-century craft, of wood
Straining against ropes, sails unfurling
Like wings to set ships flying across these waters;
To the forgers of steel, boilers and cylinders
In the bowels of the steamships and mighty Lakers,
At rest and peaceful now in this graveyard
Of Lake Ontario.

Today no evidence of ships or yards
That built them, a lone locomotive,
The Sir John A., lies beached beside
The tourist centre, all that's left
Of that mercantile line carrying goods
To distant places.
No sense that sailors came ashore
Here for comfort in churches
And hotels, a way of life sunk
Into oblivion like their ships,
Gone, lost, and forgotten.

Here on the shore of the lake
I discover a multitude of memorials
Overlooking this imitation sea, yet
Not one to the men who navigated its waters.
Behind me young trees and park benches
Commemorate dead husbands, children
And grandparents, wives and friends. I sit
On a bench dedicated to Monique McKeller

Always remembered by her husband
Who declines to leave his name; a sweet
Red maple overshadows the Plunketts,
Tom and Edith; there's Jack Montgomery
Gisby, his living monument
Shriveled to a dry, grey stick; twice born
With the planting of that tree, now twice dead.

Mine was a weekly pilgrimage to this great
Lake's shore, an urgency set the pace
To recover that openness across the water,
Internal compass in desperate search
Of those points by which self is mapped
Life navigated. I would arrive breathless
With anticipation, sink to my knees
In relief. Sunlight and wind on water, leaves
Waving from trees. Here I sought comfort,
Having traveled far from my prairie inland sea,
Sprawling space spilling across all the margins,
The only landscape where I can truly breathe,
Where I'm all wind and light and sky, yet
Anchored like a deeply rooted tree.

Four Short Poems

Wind

Wind lifts and arranges leaves,
soft elegant fingers
turning pages on a sultry afternoon.

New Moon

Rosy-complexioned
infant moon lies on her back
laughing up at the stars.
Caught off guard, saturnine clouds
swallow her whole.

Vines

Vines stretch out black, shiny fingers
hand pressed flat against the rough stone
wall. In the moonlight bare trees blossom
into silver. Moon, sole companion, follows me home.

Sadness

Sadness meanders
Like a muddy river.

Wind whispers, It is
Enough! It is enough!

Declarations
Slap against the shore.

The voice of history and
Presumptuous explanations.

Late Bloomer

You took all summer.

Potted flowers I bought
in the spring sat
dormant on the fire escape
through gentle rains
and hot, hazy days while
all around trees burst
into leaf, and below,
in the garden, tulips
and daffodils, peonies and
cosmos rushed headlong
to glory.

You sat still
unperturbed,
your ragged foliage
upturned and smiling
while fruits withered
on the vine, leaves
browned and curled,
you emerged, round
tight buds at first,
then a steady unfolding:
tiny white petals,
luminous centers, a
plethora of suns
fringed by a blazing corona.

Now grey day crowds in
around you, punishing wind
rises. You hold on. Wintry
nights press close,
time is short, but oh!
so precious, you
white queen of the moonlight
bearing your white chrysanthemum
truth ancient as Confucius
ubiquitous as the wind
are rooted to your place
high above the garden
of those blackened, impassioned
flowers.

I Didn't Count On This

I didn't count on this:

A riot
of colour

in the rain
red leaves

gleaming
the last

green
of summer

pushing thru
the ache

of impending
winter storms

II
The Trace in the Mind

I hate and I love: why I do you may well ask.
— Catullus (C. 84 - C. 55),
Carmina No. 85

All our failures are ultimately failures in love.
— Iris Murdoch,
<u>The Bell</u> (1958)

Prototype

You dropped out of my life like a stone.
Now you're back - okay,
let's see where that goes, and
the other
back too in a manner but
clumsy and non-committal though
surfacing from time-to-time
Who knows why? Yet
it's a pattern, this
boomerang effect,
every time I sigh
Good riddance

Haiku

Snowflakes - sudden squall
Memories quicken:
Drifts pile up at the door

Hast 'ou seen the rose

"Magnetic particles found in our brains," the headline said,
splinters of magnetite drawing us we know not where.
No mere metaphoric mandala, a literal lodestone
gathering matter like rose petals around our psychic core.

I pluck petals of memory to discover what I know of you.
I looked up to you, watched you work in the garden,
preferring always to be out of doors with you. There was
strength in your hands and healing when you touched wild things.

You laughed, petted the dog, carried babies in your arms,
always talking then, masking the silence and the stillness
carved deep within you, spaces vast and grand
as the prairie that used to be your home.

Drawing matter like rose petals around your psychic core,
fragments gather strength at the still dark centre while
petals fold, one by one, against the failing light.

Hunger

My mouth closes on the word:

It is ripe fruit, whole,

Heavy, sweet; I take it all

In, the whole thing, a burst

Of sweetness, exaltation;

My lips meet

In a song; it's a poem, a

Mantra, a prayer:

Your name, your name.

A Lunatic's Love Song

> Swear not by the moon.
> – William Shakespeare, Romeo and Juliet (1595)

To be such a fool
for beauty:
cascades of light
spilling across
a midnight sky,
the full moon a bird
of bright silver
unfurling its wings
against the darkness.

And you.

Memory
of sea-blue eyes shot through
with sunlight, your body
nestled in a sea of grass.
I lie beside you,
empty arms outstretched,
reaching for the moon.

The Trace in the Mind

In your eyes I saw mine,
flecks of gold swimming
in azure blue, liquid marble
slowly circling the dark centre.

That first summer we lay
under the sun amidst the asphodels,
sky blazed blue, I saw it all
with a crystal clarity.

But in the end it's the quality
of affection that carves the trace
in the mind. Pound said that:

I think of you all the time I read him.
I don't know why, perhaps
 it is his music which shuts me out too.

"de mis solidades vengan"
(out of solitude let them come)

And that skinny little drunk who got run over by a truck
staggering down the middle of the road dead drunk -
Tony that weasel wheezed, If you'd lose thirty pounds
off your ass you'd be good lookin'. And he stole my fish,
my antique fish pin from China, whose fins flashed
silvery blue like the tail of a mermaid, he hid it
on his body and wouldn't give it back. And you shrieked,
How can you read that fucking communist! though
you'd never read her yourself you didn't like her
politics, she'd murdered your Tibetan friends, you screamed,
ranted and raved two inches from my face until Michael
burst out laughing. I laughed too and couldn't stop
watching you in a landscape so foreign to my own.

      It's only a book, I tried to say,
not knowing then the stubborn power of the word,
indispensable and dangerous, not knowing yet
that writing is an act decisive as murder.

The Homecoming

Back from Tibet
you were changed, eyes

the colour of cornflowers.
I missed that blaze of blue

spelling out laughter
and defiance; sadness

and fear had crept in
to take their place. That

surprised me, I thought
so little of myself.

You Couldn't Have Known

You couldn't have known what explosions
        you set off in me—

Couldn't know your thoughts
ate through my skull like worms—

That your gaze, dull and cold
as steel in winter, froze my flesh—

Though I stood there before you—
        benumbed, inert, stupefied.

Denial

Today your playacting was so transparent
I was tempted to claw at your face
until the mask came off.

Watching you read Lawrence I wondered
What for? If you understood him
you wouldn't withhold yourself so systematically.

I have become an expert on deferred desire:
Unopened book, coffee grown cold
on the counter, the neatly made bed.

Love Is Like Death

There is a terrible beauty in you, a
dark dazzling place where you
harbour evil, clutch it fiercely
to yourself and refuse to let it go.

It is punishment for all
those sins you committed,
you say, and for which
you beg my pardon.

Yet you hold yourself still
retreat to that space
just behind your eyes,
dare me to forgive you.

It's not the end of the world,
you say. I say Love is like
death: it cannot be understood
or explained
yet there is a release, an unnatural
stillness, an uneasy peace
in its finality.

Logos

Some poems spiral.
others are
leaps
       from rock
              to
                      rock
in an ocean
ceaselessly changing.
Images
fade like
the whispers of trees
or burn so deep
they are always within touch
of the mind's fingers.
       I like to listen
to the poets' gentle banter
or hear them thunder
their exaltation
clear across the ages.
              I love the poets
whose truth seeps through
the cage of the printed word
like Christ's blood
through the shroud of Turin.

Now I know the shroud is a fake,
poets don't speak, only
their words do,
and truth can be as elusive
as the minds which create it;
yet I still believe in them,
these poems and the poets
who made them, more than you:
Your flesh never held me
so close as their word.

Bonded Not

Bonded not
by love –
Pain – sound
of tearing flesh,
gush of blood,
the baby's cry.

Desert Bloom

You were *the phantom*
of the man-who-would-understand.
The first time I saw you
a current flowed
beneath the cage of your body
I imagined myself
slipping in
becoming
one with you.

Over time you taught me
to despise my body,
passion, sex - I learned
to forge them all into weapons
and turn them against myself.

Utter Destruction
Total Waste
The desert-of-myself
that-would-not-flower:
I waited for the seed
to come from you.

Mythology of Love undeniable seduction.

That was before I was smashed
into a thousand mirrored fragments
every one
a reflection of you.

This Yearning

The way you look
at me I can tell
you think I haven't

noticed. *Doesn't care*
Lets herself go
Given up

Those thoughts
flit across your face
like shadows

on stagnant water.
Not Life, I want
to say, Men,

but our relationship
isn't so intimate as that.
Anyway,

it's the inexorable struggle
against the role: you know,
2000 years of false images?

But I can tell
by your
gaze

you fancy yourself
a better judge
of what woman is.

This yearning you sense
in my body, this desire,
you read it all wrong:

I long to walk off the stage,
it says, For once
let me be.

Triptych

1.

At the bus depot

I hand the kids
off to you

like a baton
at a relay race.

You look me over
for the first time

in a year.
I cringe under

your scrutiny
(so fat, so old)

the bare facts
(poor, unemployed,

frustrated, bereft)
no amount of explanation

can refute.

I'm worn not thin
but to a frazzle,

a fire raging
but I'm not consumed,

flames dampened
by copious amounts

of food and drink
instead. I'd love

to be ravaged, I think,
to glow from within,

illuminated,
incandescent,

like a saint
beatific,

I'd turn my face
on you

and shine,
like the full moon.

2.

You gave in to biology and circumstance,
slept through it all with a dazed and silly grin.
Ten years too late, those little nameless, unremembered
acts of kindness and of love. Never conceived,
never imagined, even. Nothing to build, then,
nothing to glue it all together. You've become
your mother, married her too, settled comfortably
into the lie, let them feed you full
of your own delusions.
I liked you better in a rage, spittle flying
from the corners of your mouth,
a bag of apples smashed to pulp
against the kitchen wall.

3.

Now we exchange sleeping bags
in deserted parking lots late
on Christmas night. Clothes
next, toys, and then the kids,
barely a glance or word
between us, except for routine
reminders about bedtime
medications and cautionary
tales of slippery roads. I
keep my head down, concentrating
on the business at hand, you
fade in and out of the shadows,
your naked piano fingers
gleaming in the moonlight
like ivory keys, glint
of the gas station lights
on your glasses the only
solid fact about you.
I wonder when it happened
you transferred
your loyalties to here—
this town, this job, this wife.
Was it as easy as shifting
weight from one foot to the other?
I remain out here in the darkness
staking a claim to the periphery
of our lives, to this space, all
that's left of our intersecting lives,
this breathing space, that rises
from infinity, hearkens me home.

There's a Funeral Here Today

There's a funeral here today.
Four black crows in a brown
Field beside the garden of
Yellow bearded iris brood
Beneath a blank blue sky.

Black, for the endless Night that
Cradles you;
Brown, for Mother Earth
To whom you must return;
Yellow, for your faith and constancy;
Blue, for your trust in Heavenly Grace.

There's a funeral here today.
A shiny black hearse sits out front
Of the brownstone chapel, pale
Jonquils fill the hall. I wear blue.

Black,
For the midnight gloom of sorrow
Shutting out all light and joy;
Brown, for the dullness of days
Now that you are gone;
Yellow, for the fear with which
I face tomorrow;
Blue (Your eyes were blue)
I am drowned in blue,
Most unholy blue!
Incessantly, inconsolably blue.

Elegy

> *Use your light and return to the source*
> *of light. This is called practicing eternity.*
> — Lao-Tsu, <u>Tao Ta Ching</u>

Since you died,
the first full moon.
Otherworldly light
spills across the sea, the sky,
unearthly, faery, godly
gossamer light.
I imagine you are that bright
diaphanous shroud, covered
with light as with a garment
stretching out the heavens
like a curtain.

Below, waves like the backs
of whales you loved
undulate, gather light
and travel into shore, a
pod of playful giants;
you in unison dancing
upon the face of the brooding
deep, your shining spirit
unfurling heavenly wings
and rolling away the darkness.

No! you haven't sunk
into oblivion like a stone -
here you are still, a fiery bird
flaming upon the waters.

I believe in a Power Greater Than Myself: It's Not Always Kind

I think of him as a smaller, darker more sensitive
version of you, as someone who was desperately afraid
of exposing his vulnerability but compelled to show it
anyway, whose emotions showed up in his face
because it was no good his trying to hide them. I wonder
if he wasn't the brother I would have preferred

I hardly spoke to you but was conscious of your every move
as you swam in and out of my peripheral vision, always
aware of the low rumble of your voice like thunder
way off in the distance on the eve of a summer storm

You spoke of his death matter-of-factly,
it had done you good, led to a sort of epiphany,
you turned to face the wave of your grief
and discovered time had stood still, time
had lain down with your dead brother, stretched
out horizontally, infinitely, in every direction

You smiled. His death brought you peace now
you know it's true: Life is One. Equal. Eternal.
Everlasting. In the darkening hallway, you smiled.

Past Hope

When all hope was gone
I thought love would fly too

but it hangs on stubbornly
refusing to listen to reason.

Dreams

Of all places
you were in my dreams.

What subterranean impulses
surfaced and pulled you in?

I awoke to the setting moon
and you

slipping below the horizon.

Weather

Rain. Finally. Parched trees
revive a little, grass turns
from straw-yellow to pale green.
I breathe a little easier
for the first time in days, at last
momentary relief, a slight lifting
of heat and humidity that cloyed
like an unwelcome lover.
St. Martin's Bells on the balcony hang
dejectedly, sodden with
the insistent drizzle; bedraggled
cats slouch sullenly in the kitchen
and trees, saturated now, shed
their leaves under the weight
of falling water.

This is the tail-end of Hurricane Dennis,
forces from afar we can't escape—
like you
in my dreams again last night you
brought me not a bunch but a tree
of roses taller than you, roots
kept fresh in a giant glass of water and
a warning: Don't plant it, it won't grow.
I didn't ask why you appeared, where
your wife might be, happy to have you
here in the kitchen entertaining
the kids like old times I wear paisley
silk pyjamas slippery and cool
against my skin, remembering
the fit of our bodies generating
our own weather system — a storm
at first, like Dennis,
then a gentle blessing
like this rain.

III

When I Think On Your Lives

Other people affect you: It's really no more complicated than that.
— Richard Ford,
A Multitude of Sins (2002)

When I Think On Your Lives

When I think on your lives
I recall an experiment
in social psychology
where dogs are made to leap
over a bar, the obstacle
set low at first and easy to clear, then raised
with another order to jump and
the sequence repeated
until the bar is too high
for any dog, yet
orders still come, commands
to master a height which
by virtue of their being
they cannot attain.
And so the dogs lie down, finally,
panting, resigned,
having recognized the futility
of their efforts.
Now a new phase of the research begins:
the bar's lowered, then lowered again
until it's so close to the ground
a spider could spring over it
but the dogs refuse
to even try
to overcome
the barrier

When I reflect on your lives
I remember a joke
about a psychologist
who teaches a spider to
clear a miniature high-jump,
and at each successive leap
the doctor pulls off a leg
to see how the insect will manage,
records the result in his notebook,
then barks out the order again:
Jump, spider! Jump!
two, three, finally all eight legs are plucked,
the spider's round, stolid body
stripped of all possible means of movement
lying inert and flush to the ground.
Jump, spider, jump!
the professor demands one more time
and when the creature doesn't move
writes in his notebook
that the spider, at the removal
of its eighth and last leg,
finally lost its hearing.

When I consider your lives
I hear the narrator of *The Mill on the Floss*
saying there's a certain class of people
who can afford to have morals
(no mention of that wealthier class
who can afford not to have any)
and then there's you -
reduced to the level of survival
you can't afford to have morals but then
you can't afford not to
because you're under the bell jar and
in that particular light with a certain perspective
anybody is going to look bad

When I think on your pain
I recollect an image from
The Stone Angel
see a corral strung with barbed wire
and a cow penned in so close
no matter which way she turns
she backs into the barbs:
no matter how hard she tries
to keep clear of the fence
her flanks get pricked,
and bleed

When I contemplate your struggles
I envisage Prometheus
bound to a storm-beaten rock
abandoned to the intolerable present
inexorably grinding him down; of
Sisyphus forever fated to roll a rock uphill
which eternally rolls back to crush him;
I think of Job bearing up under the afflictions
heaped upon him;
of Frankenstein's innocent creation
made monstrous

When I imagine your dreams I know
they're no different from my own: a little
room to grow, a little space to breathe,
some colour and movement
to relieve this static grey,
a chance for our kids to turn out all right,
cries to be heard, smiles returned,
a contribution to the world
not beyond
our wildest dreams.

Collateral Damage: April 2003

The Iraqis are sick people and we are the chemotherapy.
– American Corporal Ryan Dupre [1]

(Add to this, cluster bombs and
uranium-tipped missiles, ancient sites
reduced to rubble, burning cities and
no water, thirteen years of sanctions,
a million children dead, the rest
weakened by illness and by hunger.
Thousands of war-wounded
stream to hospitals long-exhausted
of their supplies, hospitals deprived
by the sanctions of bandages
and painkillers, disinfectant
and aspirin. Bereft of food, electricity
and water, of currency, government
and priceless treasures marking ten
thousand years of culture, citizens wait,
less patiently now, for the billions of dollars
in humanitarian goods promised
by the U.S., approved by the U.N.,
and already paid for by Iraq.) [2]

Consider this: Praising coverage
of the war, Roger Mosey, head
of the BBC television news, says
*it almost feels like World Cup football
when you go from [one place]
to another theatre of war
someplace else, and you're
switching between battles.* [3]

Was he thinking of this scene:
Horrified soldiers witnessing
coalition comrades blown
apart by rocket-propelled grenades,
their legs dangling by a tangle of sinews?
Did he zoom in on that one particular soldier
sobbing uncontrollably, cradling
a chunk of unrecognizable human flesh,
desperate for a safe place to hide
the remains of his friend, determined
that at least this piece of him shall be
salvaged, buried, and mourned? [4]
Or was it the interview with that
U.S. sergeant who killed the female
civilian standing next to an Iraqi
soldier? *I'm sorry*, he said, *but
the chick got in the way.* [5]

Maybe it was the bridge in Nasariyah,
the one Fox news anchor and all-around
know-nothing Shepard Smith still
can't pronounce correctly
after ten days of war. Unsure
whether they were friend or foe,
U.S. troops unloaded on civilians
fleeing the war zone:
killed twelve, *one a little girl*
no older than five, a Times of London
reporter noted, and clothed in a pretty
orange and gold dress. [6]
She lies dead in a ditch
next to the body of a man who
may be her father. And perhaps
it's her mother over there in a battered
old Volga peppered with ammunition holes,
slumped in the back seat - dead. Nearby
a father, baby girl, and boy are motionless
in a shallow grave; on the bridge itself,
nestled against the carcass of his donkey,
lies a slain Iraqi man.

Alive on the bridge, another sort of casualty:
an American soldier stained with the blood
of these dead. Lieutenant Matt Martin,
choking back tears, asks the *Times* reporter,
Did you see all that? Did you see that little baby girl?
and explains that his wife had given birth to their third
child, a daughter, while he was headed for the Gulf.
It really gets to me, Martin says, to see children
being killed like this. [7]

Elsewhere children hold up
tiny hands in terror while American
troops put rifles to their parents' heads, forcing
them to kneel in the street. [8] In Basra, a middle-
aged man is carried to hospital in blood-soaked
pyjamas, [9] bodies pile up in the mortuary, [10]
and British soldiers smash their way into a
home. A mother weeps and a young man
trembles in fear as he and his brothers
are manacled, hooded, and marched
into the street, prisoners of war. [11]

Collateral damage: soldiers like Martin caught
again by the *old Lie*, [12] sacrificed by agents
of death, capitalizers of misery, the usurers Pound
identified and deplored, [13] who don't wear uniforms,
speculate on the price and profit by the cost
of war. Nothing sweet or fitting [14]: not liberation
but occupation, no grateful Iraqis rushing to thank
and embrace him. Just smoldering resentment erupting
into demonstrable hate with their newly-exercised
freedom of speech. *He [should] have known, he
could have guessed* [15] and now something vital
has been wounded, something precious shattered; [16]
he's *transformed utterly*, [17] clenches his sullied
hands into tight fists and hides them deep
in his pockets, thinks of his baby back home,
the girl by the bridge.

Telling Stories

Live your life right, just like a story. That's the best we can do,
I suppose, although we're only telling stories. I wonder

what it means to get at the truth, if it's possible, why
we go to such pains to get it right or to hide it. I wonder

why I remember the things that I do, what I've forgotten
how much has been lost. Like Janus, two-faced god,

guardian of portals, patron of beginnings and endings,
you stand between two doors, past and future, drawing
the circle closed.

First Memories

In a scant one hundred years more
than innocence has been lost. I envy
the blank canvas you had to draw
your life upon, the empty pages you could fill.
I was born into a twisted mass of steel, dark
pavement and white noise, sprawling
cities which blot out the landscape,
machines with a will of their own.

I do not have a first memory of you.
Remember Grandmother, wizened old woman of the prairie
speaking a language I couldn't understand. But her laughter
was easy to read, those raisin eyes hidden in folds, candy
dish pushed a little further toward me with each exclamation
of Bitte! Bitte! The way her knotted hands clasped and
unclasped her cane spoke worlds. Can
still see her in a cotton print dress, cheap
turquoise sunhat tied under her chin, hanging
onto your arm as she shuffles up the sidewalk, knees bowed
under the weight of her eighty-odd years.

I remember the smell of lipstick and powder that was Mother,
red lipstick and a soft red sweater, silky blond hair brushing
my cheek, a softness like flowers, gentleness like rain.

But you. I cannot see your face or feel your touch. You
come to me as a voice, deep and wide as a river, the
low rumble of boulders tumbling along the riverbed,
the steady pulse of a current overhead.

Misreadings

A shock of white hair
eyes squinting into the sun:
a photo of
you at five years old
alone in a harvested cornfield
searching the emptiness of the sky.

Here you are at seventy-five
hair again white, eyes squinting
through the effort of old age
desperate to script your own death,
remembering your grandparents
begging for oblivion, cancer
scuttling through their veins

After a lifetime of betrayal your
body's not likely to oblige; yours
was nothing to show off or count on
even as a young girl. What is it like
to inhabit a body, to feel at home?
Sign and signified one, an ideogram
or stark hieroglyphic providing
a clue as to what's inside

You resisted all those versions
of yourself imposed on you by others,
all those misreadings made you open
your eyes wide: such incongruities! An
arch of the eyebrow, curve of a hip,
words? what map of the human heart
was this? They made you laugh
at first
until the weight of them, the steady
cumulative drop mounted like stones
to shut out the sky. You stopped
measuring the space between
images: deep was the sound, hollow
as a sepulchre's door. Imperceptible,
insubstantial as a shadow now
you slip through any crack
fit any shape
offered to you

At the Laundromat

I can see,
when I pull them out
of the dryer in full view
of everybody,
like that woman over there
at the table next to mine,
her sheets folded neatly
and piled up whiter
than white,
pastel t-shirts
and designer pants
blocked into packages
like they're still
in the box,
I can see,
her fine blond hair neatly
tied back, porcelain
skin flawless, her
immaculate clothes
hugging her trim little body,
I can see
how I've let them
all go, these
vestments, faded and
threadbare, their
edges unraveling—

As You Turn

As you turn to wave
a shadowy form changes

shape like a cloud
in your ten-year-old body

escaping momentarily
into a sardonic grin.

It takes even your mouth
by surprise.

There it is, lurking behind
light-brown eyes the clear

tawny colour of a still
rock-bottom, sun-lit stream.

Your thin and fragile
frame struggles

against the knowledge
of this adult understanding,

it throws you off-balance
and you turn away

with the faltering gait
of an uncertain kid.

At the Post Office

At the Post Office
people are stealing furtive glances
at the person ahead of me in line.
They are of all types, the glimpses,

curious and embarrassed, amused,
incredulous, malicious and hateful.
Postal workers openly smirk.
The object, desperately oblivious,
stares straight ahead and hugs
the leather purse that matches

her leather pumps more tightly
to her breast. She has
shoulder-length, blonde hair
which curls under slightly,

glasses and a cotton-print
dress. I don't like to stare:
it takes me a while to figure out
what the fuss is about.

It's her turn now. Behind
the counter two male workers
exchange school-boy confidences, choke
back a giggle and catch the eye
of their supervisor who picks up
their signal and walks by, her heels
wobbling under her weight, heaving
with stifled laughter as the blonde
makes her way to the front.

All watch from behind,
strain eyes and ears
for the exaggerated wiggle,
the falsetto tones of her voice.

A Matter of Time

        barrelling down the information highway   bound
for god knows where   no going back, no slowing down
looking for a pit stop   desperate now
    can't find a ramp or exit   anywhere

        electronic messages course through my brain
I'm a tuning fork   a steady, reedy whine

      never let up, never wind down   rush

& push   noise   garbage cars
        whizzing past
            me
        here on the corner

(this corner – every corner—a power struggle)

me on the corner   still waiting   so angry
            I want to hurl

something
the way I really did
that day the car came screeching
round the corner in the pouring rain
nearly knocking us to the four corners
of the apocalypse, my kids & I,
missing my son by an inch, a mere inch
& I'm so angry I'm smashing
my umbrella into the windshield, my
kids tugging at my sleeve (*mom! mom!*)
me screaming, *we're walking here!*
we're walking here! like Rizzo
in Midnight Cowboy, & for a moment
I'm inside his skin, hunched
& bleeding, knowing
where I'll finally end up:
It's only a matter of time

Desire Being Their Birthright

Sun rose this morning
a luminous red ball
through a mist so thick
I felt ethereal as a ghost
walking through walls
materializing magically
when droplets of dew
catching the sun's fire
clung to my flesh
like a garment.

Watched the sun
wobble its way up into
the sky as I gathered in washing
hung from the line wrinkled
and limp as the skin of old men,
bend down with the first T-shirt,
see Moppy crouched low in the grass
eyes opened wide, wild luminous,
two black-rimmed moons slashed
by a single black line.
Tom follows me in at the door
yawning and stretching, liquid
beauty, serpentine grace,
his yellow Egyptian eyes half-
closed in the mounting heat
of the new day.

On the way to school (sun
shrinking into a hot, white ball)
we greet the neighbourhood cats:
Hi kitty! Good morning, kitty, kitty, kitty!
in their familiar places at the end of the driveway,
crouched low on the step, or lengthening out
(belly exposed) against the glass of a picture window.

I nod habitual helloes
to the dour old men collapsed
in their lawn chairs, gazing
like undignified Sphinxes
across the waste of their lives,
their existence centered
on this moment of our
rounding the corner but
won't risk a greeting
or a smile, watch us
go the whole length of the block,
straining at their leashes.

These men,
whose eyes shoot out
like grappling hooks
to catch at my arm.
These men,
who steal my sympathy
without thought
of the cost.
These men,
vulnerable as mewling kittens
and as blind.

Self-Doubt

Something had shifted.
Some inner foundation
Had lurched
And begun to slide.

Imperceptible at first,
A change in the quality
Of the light or angle
Of vision, in the way
Her feet didn't feel
Quite connected when
She stepped down —hard—
On the pavement.

It began with the slightest
Hestitation, then a
Tangible space, next a gulf
Ever-widening until
She couldn't broach the distance
Between herself and the stranger
Standing off just to one side.

That stranger wears
A twisted smile, never
Stops mimicking
Her every move.

At the Welfare Office

At the welfare office I ask the receptionist how long I'll have to wait.
She smiles, *Ten minutes*, she says, but I catch the eye
of the person leaning against the counter, the woman
with the iridescent scars running up and down her arms.
Yeah, right, when Hell freezes over, she scoffs, loud enough
for everybody to hear. I sit beside the young woman holding down
a squirming toddler, a wailing baby in her arms. *She's hungry,*
she apologizes, *we've been waiting for over an hour.*

This is bullshit! a young man spits out as he strides to the desk,
the baby's cries faltering for a moment. *I want to see my worker, I've
been waiting all fucking day!*

I told you, the receptionist says evenly, not bothering to get up
from her chair set well back from the plexiglass barrier,
there's no one to see you, you already got your cheque...

But I used it to pay rent, for chrissakes! the man explodes,
to buy food. I told you! My housemates kicked me out!

I can't issue a new cheque, the worker says wearily,
there's nothing I can do.

*Don't you understand? Shit! I need money for a new place,
I need vitamins...*

Then you'll have to MAKE them take you back...

They're not going to! the young man shouts,
The Beautiful Young Man of Alabaster Skin and Golden Curls
even an angel would envy, *they'd just as soon beat the piss out of me,
I've got AIDS, they don't want me near them!* and he slumps against
the counter muttering that he's not leaving, not if he has to stay all day,
all fuckin' night, fuckin' forever, he's not going until he gets his cheque.

The woman across the way – she looks like Miss Chatelaine with her
carefully coiffed hair, her make-up and beige pumps – is chatting
to her neighbour about school and the weather, how Bell has cut off
her phone again, how the kids don't sleep at night, complain about
everything she does even when she goes out of her way,
bends over backwards and overextends her budget. *My lawyer says
when I choose to get off welfare I can sue my husband for more support.
Choose? I said to him. Choose?!*

There's the Lady of the Scars still draped across the counter. She wears
the wounds of the spirit on the outside, writing on the body, her own brand.
Anger gouged into fleshy surfaces, a visceral hieroglyphics of
anguish and despair. No beauty in this, no compromise, and no apology either.

I'm slouched in my chair listening to the voices in this room,
wrestling with the knowledge that our lives are an open book
to be examined, judged, mocked, denied…I sit, swallowing
the collective pain in great gasping gulps and clamp down hard
on my rage.

Remember the Days

Remember the days
when friends would
arrive, journey up three
floors to our attic
apartment, a nest of
worn Persian carpets,
portly cushions
hugging gaily
garlanded walls,

&
we'd sit – just sit—
for hours and hours
smoking hand-rolled
cigarettes, drinking
chamomile tea,
our Siamese
kittens purring
to the dulcet tones of Judy
Collins or the twanging
sound collages of John
Fahey's solo string-
plucked steel guitar;

we'd think there was no tomorrow
& there wasn't, not really, just
you & the eyes across the room,
the music & our laughter
taking precedence over words,

a sideways glance or a smile
all the protection we'd seek
against the insolent sun
making its relentless descent
through the moribund sky

But I'm Hungry

Poverty, Mahatma Gandhi said,
is the worst form of violence.
Not many get that. She didn't either
until tight in its grip her world shrunk
to this tiny, dark box where she's crushed
together with her two small children,
everywhichway she turns, there
is something to block her; every
time she raises herself up, someone
is there to knock her back down. She
remembers the first time she wanted
to slap her toddler hard: he reached
for the milk and tipped it over, all
they had left until the next cheque day;
Nothing to do but cry over spilt milk,
huddled together she wailed and he howled,
heads hanging, two blue figures in a fixed
landscape, her stomach turning at the thought
of going to the food bank or drop-in for more;
she can't face their questions, that look—
pity or condemnation —both
cause her hands to sweat, a
collapsing of her innards, the loss
of her voice. In the beginning
she expected kindness, actually waited
for a call: *Are your kids okay?* they'd ask.
How are you coping? They'd acknowledge
what she was going through instead of justifying
their own impotence by pointing a finger at her,
recognize who she is, not equate her
with her diminished circumstances.

Now she tries never to expect
or ask for anything—
it betrays a weakness and a cause for blame, like
that time she went to welfare with a black eye
and the worker told her if she couldn't protect
herself she couldn't protect her children and
he was obliged to notify the authorities
who could. She turned right around
and walked out, even though
she needed help, her ex had punched holes
in all her apartment walls, rifled through
her purse and took what cash she had.

That's when she shut herself and her kids
up in their cramped, hot apartment, put
the old bicycle locks on the cupboard
and fridge doors so her older boy
wouldn't eat the little food that was left.
Even when he cried, *But I'm hungry,
mummy*, she told him to wait for his supper,
sat still and cold as stone, calculating
how long the food would last if she ate less,
if she went without, wondering how
she got this way, how long
she could manage, when it happened
that she lost herself irrevocably...
Once upon a time
she had inhabited a vast open landscape:
she remembers colour and motion,
whispers and radiant light,
an inner world like a mighty forest
or an endless sea

They Picked Up My Son

I can't think about it.
A boy,
your son,
in pieces on the road.
Tufts of light brown hair
ground into the windshield,
an abandoned ball cap, an
empty pair of running shoes.
Your son,
in pieces on the road. An
arm, a leg, slabs of flesh
flung against the pavement,
into ditches, and
across the field where
they found his face
severed clean from the skull,
a startled mask staring
straight up to heaven.
Your son,
in pieces on the road.
Fingernails shattered
by the force of the blow:
a boy on a bicycle, a
drunk driver,
& police
gagging on the remains,
but gathering them,
for you, for the father
restrained behind the rope.
They picked up your son
piece by piece.

He lies in his coffin now
stitched together
like Frankenstein's monster.
All you want is a hug,
one last embrace, a send-off
to bear him safely
on his final journey home.
Only his hands,
they caution you, Touch
only his hands, & so
you gather up
his long, slender fingers,
cradle them gently
like the prelapsarian petals
of some rare, exotic flower,
Gather them up, lest he fall
to pieces in your arms.

On the Beach

Far away across the water
(the colour of peacock feathers)

Your disembodied head
(black in the shadow

of the billion-year-old cliffs which rise
out of the water like the truck of Colossus)

Bobs like a cork. I look in your direction
(shielding my eyes from the sun) think

About waving (but aren't sure you can see
me) let my mind drift along with the current

Watch the oily surface of the water slide
Across my vision, undulate in serpentine

Motion, glisten golden and break
Into diamond-shaped patterns of light.

I've lost sight of you now (wonder
whether I should worry) turn

My attention to the laughter of children,
The barking of dogs on the beach.

On Your Birthday

I don't remember how we first met.
What I do remember is you
always being here, a skinny little
blond with bobbed hair,
blue veins showing through
skin translucent as ice
concealing a raging river

Frail as a she-waif
you looked,
but you could stride as fast
and talk as loud as the boys,
take on anybody, and
almost all met their match in you

Fear was the weakness
you refused to countenance,
always met it head-on
with the fierceness of the warrior
you loved to play best,

had little patience for me—
dark and timid as you
were fair and strong. How you
laughed the day the boys flung
obscenities like darts
around the playground and I,
having never heard the words before,
had to ask you what they meant

You schooled me in the ways of the world,
threw me into the deep
confident I would float, held me
with your glittering eye
never loosening your grip
until I mastered a truth
finally worthy of you

Now we're grown women with children
of our own still trying to reconcile
the child within us. You've grown
sadder around the eyes, your
chiseled shoulders have been worn
to a rounded softness. They remind
me of the hills we climbed as girls,
curves as voluptuous
as a woman's body
gouged out of the prairie
by an ancient mass
of ice and snow.

It's the Laughter

It's the laughter
in the evening—
Dolores & June
sprawled in their
lawn chairs across
the street, taking
a well-deserved
rest after 70-odd
years of feminine
struggle, calling
Howdy stranger! as
I step out the door
into the lengthening
shadows of the deepening
day: it's the murmur
of their voices as I
pick tomatoes hanging
like moons; it's the
moon, high & full
racing past clouds
the colour of dust
& ripe blueberries,
the call of the geese
in V-formation, my
cats in the garden
crouched low, stalking
their neighbours; it's
the wind, the cool
lake breeze sweeping
across the land
to my yard, lifting

my clothes & my hair
with its soft, gentle
fingers, balm to
the pressing white
heat of the day: it's
gathering ripe tomatoes
like jewels in my arms,
offering the treasures
to June & Delores who
give me recipes & praise
in exchange;
it's their
asking, Do you know
what marijuana looks
like? then leading
me to the edge
of the sidewalk to
point at a plant, a
leprechaun green,
frayed-edged, three-
leafed gem springing
up from the pavement, &
me saying, It sure
looks like marijuana;
their hoots of laughter,
confessing they hadn't
believed Jason but
they do me, yet how could
it be, where did it
come from, who could
have planted the seed?
it's their warning me
in conspiratorial giggles

I might see them stumbling
& acting queer; it's
hearing their voices
fade away in the
dusk as I ascend
my apartment stairs,
tomato-laden & light-
hearted; oh, yes, it's
the laughter
in the evening.

Notes to the Poems:

Page 19, "Respite"   From "No worst, there is none" (1918) by Gerard Manley Hopkins.

Page 24, "Testimonial" From <u>Moby Dick; or The Whale</u> (1851) by Herman Melville.

Page 28, "Late Bloomer" The chrysanthemum was first cultivated in China as a flowering herb and is described in writings as early as the 15th Century B.C. The earliest illustrations of mums show them as small, yellow daisy-like flowers, and used as an herb the chrysanthemum was believed to have the power of life. The chrysanthemum was next cultivated in Japan where a single flowered chrysanthemum was adopted in the 8th century A.D. as the crest and official seal of the Emperor. From there multiple varieties of the flower spread across the globe. Since the chrysanthemum was first introduced into the United States during colonial times, its popularity has grown such that mums now reign as the undisputed "Queen of the Fall Flowers." (National Chrysanthemum Society, USA.)

Page 33, Section III. "The Trace in the Mind": See Ezra Pound, Canto LXXV:

> *nothing matters but the quality*
> > *of the affection –*
> > > *- in the end – that has carved the trace in the mind.*

Page 36, *Hast 'ou seen the rose.* Ezra Pound, Canto 74:
Hast'ou seen the rose in the steel dust
(or swansdown ever?)
so light is the urging, so ordered the dark petals of iron
we who have passed over Lethe.

Page 40, *"de mis solidades vengan"*: The title comes from Lope de Vega, by way of Ezra Pound.

Page 40, The communist: Agnes Smedley (1892-1950), American, working-class feminist, teacher, socialist and revolutionary, journalist and author. Growing up in Michigan in desperate poverty shaped her life-long commitment to the causes of the poor and the oppressed. In America, she worked with Margaret Sanger at the *Birth Control Review* in New York City and later became involved in India's fight for independence as well as the Chinese Revolution. Smedley covered the Chinese Civil War during the 1930s, travelling with the Chinese revolutionary army, and served as a correspondent for several newspapers, including *Franfuter Zeitung* and the *Manchester Guardian*. She was turned down when she applied to be a member of the Chinese Communist Party in the 1930s. Nevertheless, she remained passionately devoted to the Chinese communist cause. Smedley returned to the United States in the 1940s, then FBI accusations of spying drove her to Britain for the last years of her life. Her ashes are buried in the Baloaoshan Revolutionary Cemetery in Beijing. Smedley's books include a semi-autobiographical novel, <u>Daughter of Earth</u>, and several accounts of the Chinese Revolution.

Page 47, "Desert Bloom": *The phantom-of-the-man-who-would-undersatnd.* Adrienne Rich.

Page 52, "Triptych": William Wordsworth, "Composed a few miles above Tintern Abbey on revisiting the banks of the Wye during a tour. July 13, 1798":

On that best portion of a good man's life,
His little, nameless, unremembered, acts
Of kindness and of love.

Page 66, "Collateral Damage: April 2003"

1 - Tim Wise, *So This is What War Looks Like? ZNet Commentary*, April 2, 2003.
2 - Various media, including *ZNet Commentaries*, April 2003 and *Harper's Weekly Review*, April 22, 2003.
3 - Leaked e-mail, cited by John Pilger in *Crime Against Humanity*, ZNet Commentary, April 10, 2003.
4 - Wise, ibid.
5 - Dexter Filkins, *Either Take a Shot or Take a Chance*, New York Times, March 29, 2003, p. A1.
6 - *Times of London*, cited by Tim Wise, ibid.
7 - Wise, ibid.
8 - Pilger, ibid.
9 - Unedited Al Jazeera tape, cited by Robert Fisk, *Raw, Devastating Realities That Expose the Truth About Basra, ZNet Commentary*, April 22, 2003.
10 - Al Jazeera tape, Fisk, ibid.
11 - *Sky News*, cited by Tim Llewellyn, former BBC Middle East Correspondent, in a letter to the *Guardian*, April 2003, cited by Pilger, ibid.
12 - Wilfred Owen, *Dulce et Decorum Est*.
13 - Ezra Pound, *The Cantos*.
14 - Owen, ibid.
15 - Sebastian Faulks, *Birdsong*.
16 - Wise, ibid.
17 - W.B. Yeats, *Easter 1916*.

Acknowledgements:

Versions of the following poems were published previously: "In a Word," "The Legacy," Ash, ed., Wayne K. Spear, 3:2 (Spring 1996) ; "Hunger," "Weather," Queen's Feminist Review (QFR), vol. 8 (2000); "Triptych," QFR, vol. 11 (2003); "They picked up my son." QFR, vol. 12 (2004); "A Single Seed," QFR, vol. 13 (2005); "Late Bloomer," "It's the Laughter," Kingston Poets' Gallery," ed. Elizabeth Greene, Artful Codger Press (2006); "Natural Desires," 'Scapes, ed. Diane Dawber, Hidden Brook Press (2007); On Your Birthday," QFR, vol. 15 (2007); "But I'm hungry," The Local Harvest, a publication of The National Farmers Union, Local 316, ed. Harvey Schachter, vol. 2 (2007); "When I Think On Your Lives," Common Magic: The Book of the New, eds. Elizabeth Greene and Danielle Gugler, Artful Codger Press (2008). Versions of the following poems were performed on stage in The Garbage and the Flowers, Theatre Kingston, Kim Renders, Director: "A Conversation of Crows," "At the Welfare Office," "At the Laundromat," "A Matter of Time," and "Celestial Convergence."

Many have influenced and encouraged my writing over the years. While it's impossible to name them all, thank you to Bill Howard, Joan Givner, Saros Cowasjee, Béla Szabados, Lea Ord, Jan Hermiston, Laura Lee Orser, Janice Kirk, Anne Archer, Carla Douglas, Cheryl Sutherland, Marie Lloyd, Mary Cameron, Eric Folsom, Joanne Page, Steven Heighton, Mark Sinnett, Merilyn Simonds, Wayne Grady, Maureen Garvie, Diane Schoemperlen, Kim Renders, Jason Heroux, Kent Nussey. And to Jeanette Lynes: thank you for your sharp eye and expert suggestions. My gratitude goes to world-renowned sculptor Néle Azevedo for her generosity in allowing me to use her photograph of 'Melting Men' for the cover of my book. Special thanks to my friend and editor, Elizabeth Greene – your patience, good humour, and steadfast support made all the difference.

Biographical Sketch:

Tara Kainer grew up in Knoxville, Tennessee and Regina, Saskatchewan. She attended the University of Regina and Queen's University, Kingston and has been a long-time advocate for rights and services for the poor. She has published poetry in literary journals, including Ash, ed. Wayne Spears, and the Queen's Feminist Review; in anthologies: Kingston Poets' Gallery, Elizabeth Greene, ed. (Artful Codger Press, 2006); 'Scapes, Diane Dawber, ed. (Hidden Brook Press, 2007), and Common Magic: The Book of the New, Danielle Gugler and Elizabeth Greene, eds. (Artful Codger Press, 2009). As a member of Foxglove Collective, she co-edited On the Threshold: Writing Toward the Year 2000 (Beach Holme, 1999). She has also published essays, articles, interviews and book reviews in several newspapers, journals, and magazines, including ARC, NOISE, Quarry, and the Kingston Whig-Standard. Currently, she is employed by the Justice, Peace, & Integrity of Creation Office of the Sisters of Providence of St. Vincent de Paul in Kingston, Ontario.

Biographical Sketch of Cover Art Artist:

Néle Azevedo, lives and works in São Paulo-Brazil. Master of visual arts (Arts Institute of Sao Paulo State University) Has been working with urban interventions since 2001, with the project Minimum Monument, discussing the public monuments in the contemporary cities, such as Brasilia, Salvador, Curitiba, São Paulo, Campinas, Ribeirão Preto in Brazil end Havana (Cuba), Tokyo and Kyoto (Japan), Paris (France), Braunschweig and Berlin (Germany), Porto (Portugal), Firenze (Italy) and Stavanger (Norway).

I do interventions in public spaces in different cities and countries. Hundreds of ice sculptures are taken to central places of cities and with help from the passers-by they are left to melt. The sculptures are tiny men and women, 20 cm tall, placed on stairways. The urban intervention is called "Minimum Monument", because its meaning is tied up to the concept of the monument – it is an anti-monument.

There is a search for reconciliation between the public and private spheres, the subject and the city. In this search I've found in the pubic monument the synthesis of my uneasiness: the historical celebration far from the ordinary man. I then subverted, one by one, the characteristics of official monuments. The scale is minimal – hence the name, "Minimum Monument", there is no pedestal either hierarchy, the homage is rendered to the anonymous. The ice bodies disappear in the city, in a shared experience. The happening remains on the viewers' memories and their pictures.

After all, what motivates more is the deep love for the public spaces of cities, and the possibility of different relations that can be established there.

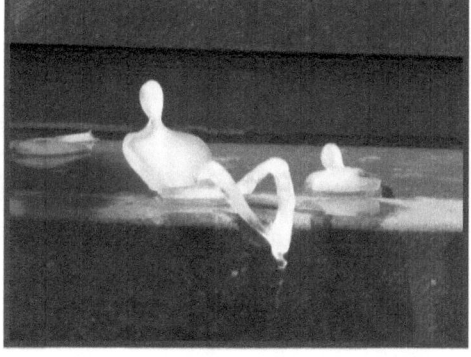

Néle Azevedo
www.neleazevedo.com.br

www.ingramcontent.com/pod-product-compliance
Lightning Source LLC
Chambersburg PA
CBHW021116080526
44587CB00010B/537